Coulda', Woulda', Did!

Ideas about the Star of Christmas

Written by P. James Freshour
Illustrated by Gail Paulus

xulon PRESS

Copyright © 2013 by P. James Freshour

Coulda', Woulda, Did!
by P. James Freshour

Printed in the United States of America

ISBN 9781628392661

All rights reserved solely by the author. The author guarantees all contents are original and do not infringe upon the legal rights of any other person or work. No part of this book may be reproduced in any form without the permission of the author. The views expressed in this book are not necessarily those of the publisher.

www.xulonpress.com

This book is dedicated to my loving wife,
Mary Kay, and to our eight grandchildren.
It is also dedicated to the memory of Melissa Rone,
a wonderful teacher and a good friend.

Introduction

A few years ago, when I was meeting with a small group of pastors, we were discussing the theories that have been proposed regarding the Star of Christmas and how it was instrumental in helping the wise men from the East locate the Christ child. Since then, I have discovered documentation that support these theories, and I have included them at the end of this book. With the help of an adult, young readers will be able to discover facts of the cosmos as well as knowledge of ancient history that relate to those events associated with this beloved Christmas story. And so, we begin the quest I have chosen to call,

"Coulda', Woulda', Did!"

P. James Freshour

If you would look up into the sky on a clear December night...you could almost see it. It's been written about, pictured on Christmas cards, and included in Christmas carols.

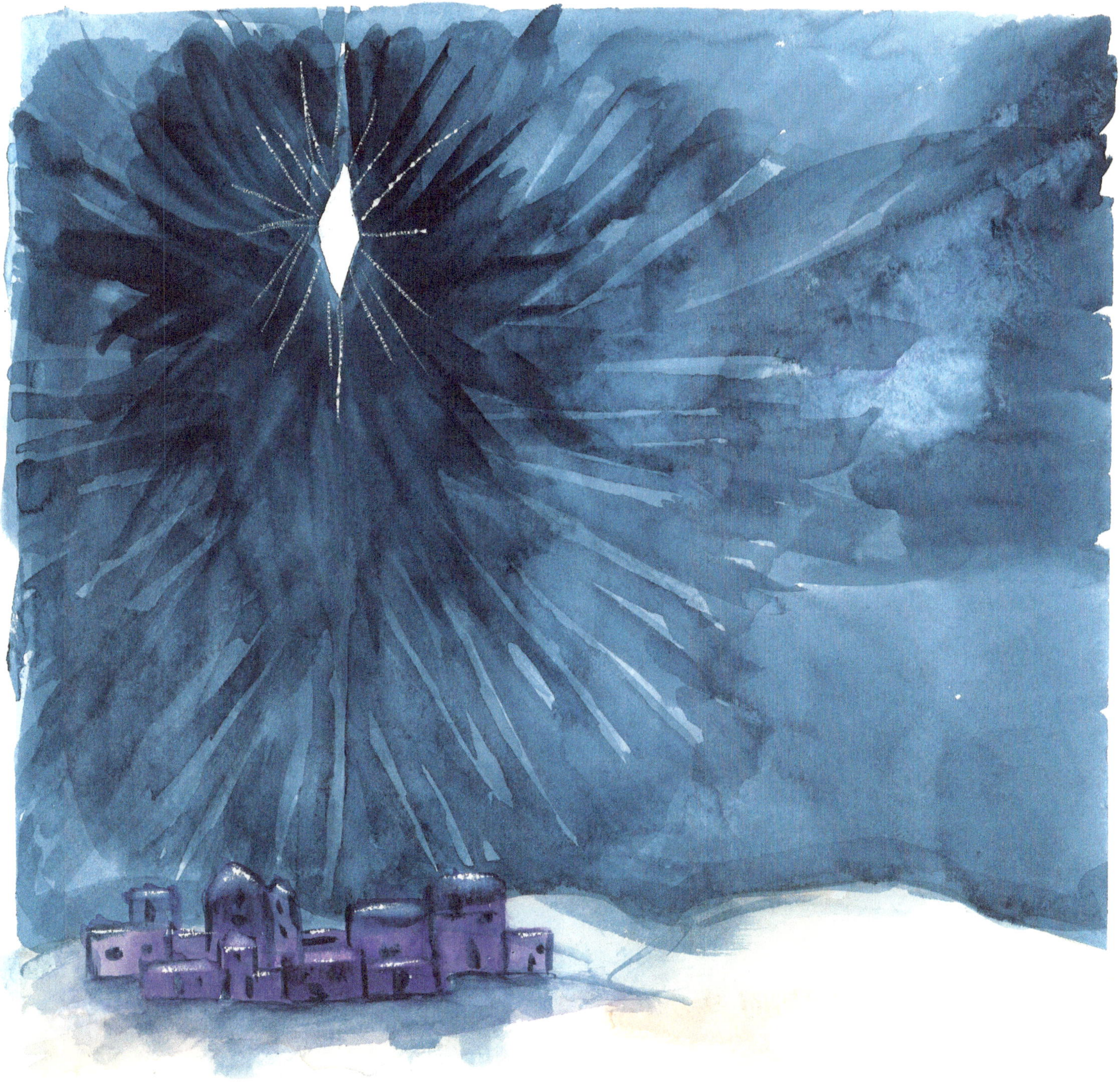

It's the star that guided the wise men to the place where the Christ child could be found so many years ago. But, how does one follow a star? How does a star "move?" And when it stops moving, where do you go from there?

These are questions that people have asked for many, many years. But we can learn that there are several different ways a star, way up in the sky, absolutely helped these visitors from the East to find our Savior.

First of all, let's understand that these visitors were special. They knew the science of the stars called **astronomy** as well as ancient interpretations of the heavens called **astrology**.

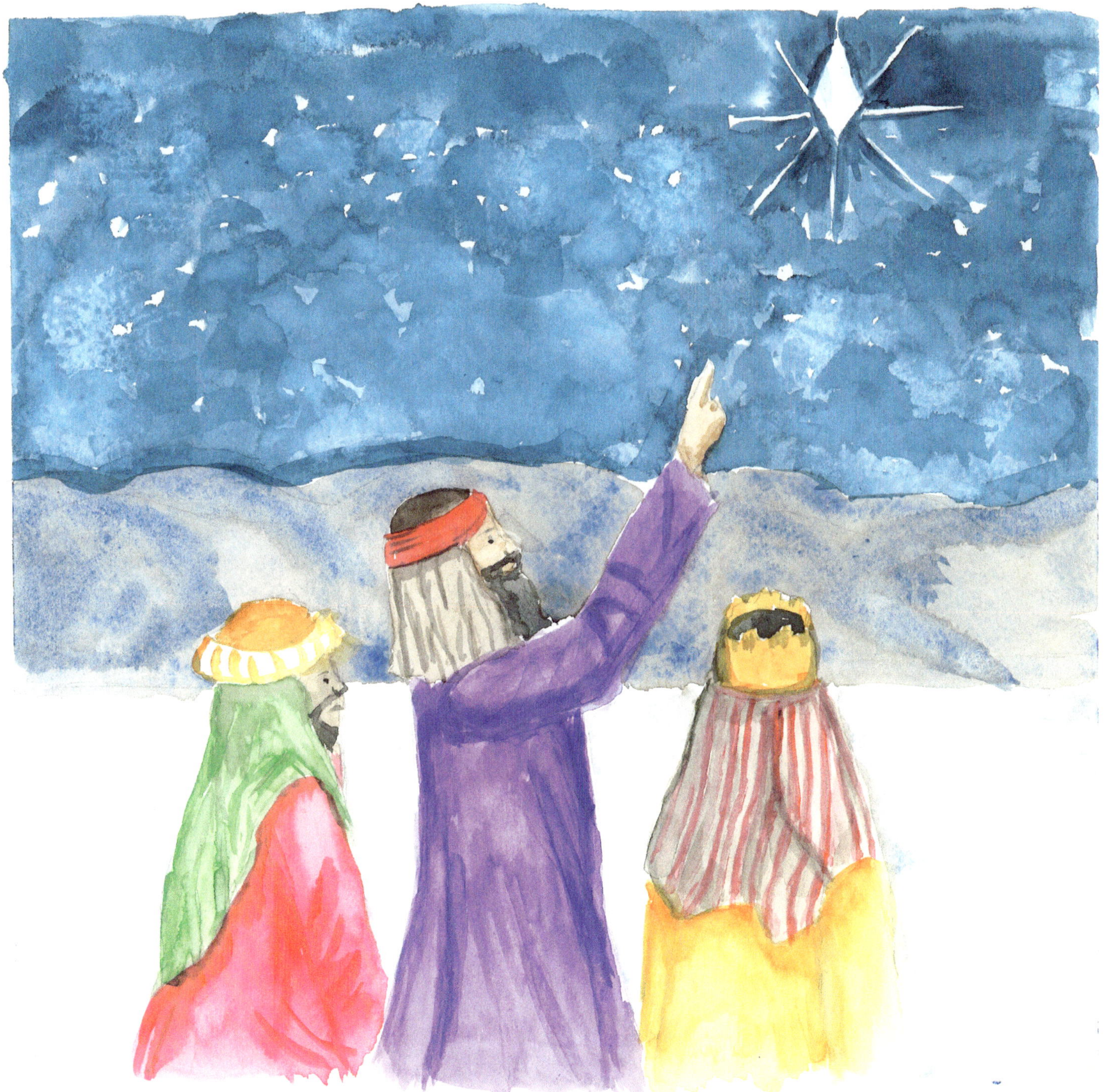

When they saw a star shining so bright one night, they knew this was a sign that a baby of royal birth had entered the world. They were convinced that they must gather some of their most important belongings together, form what is known in desert regions as a caravan, and go look for the newly born child.

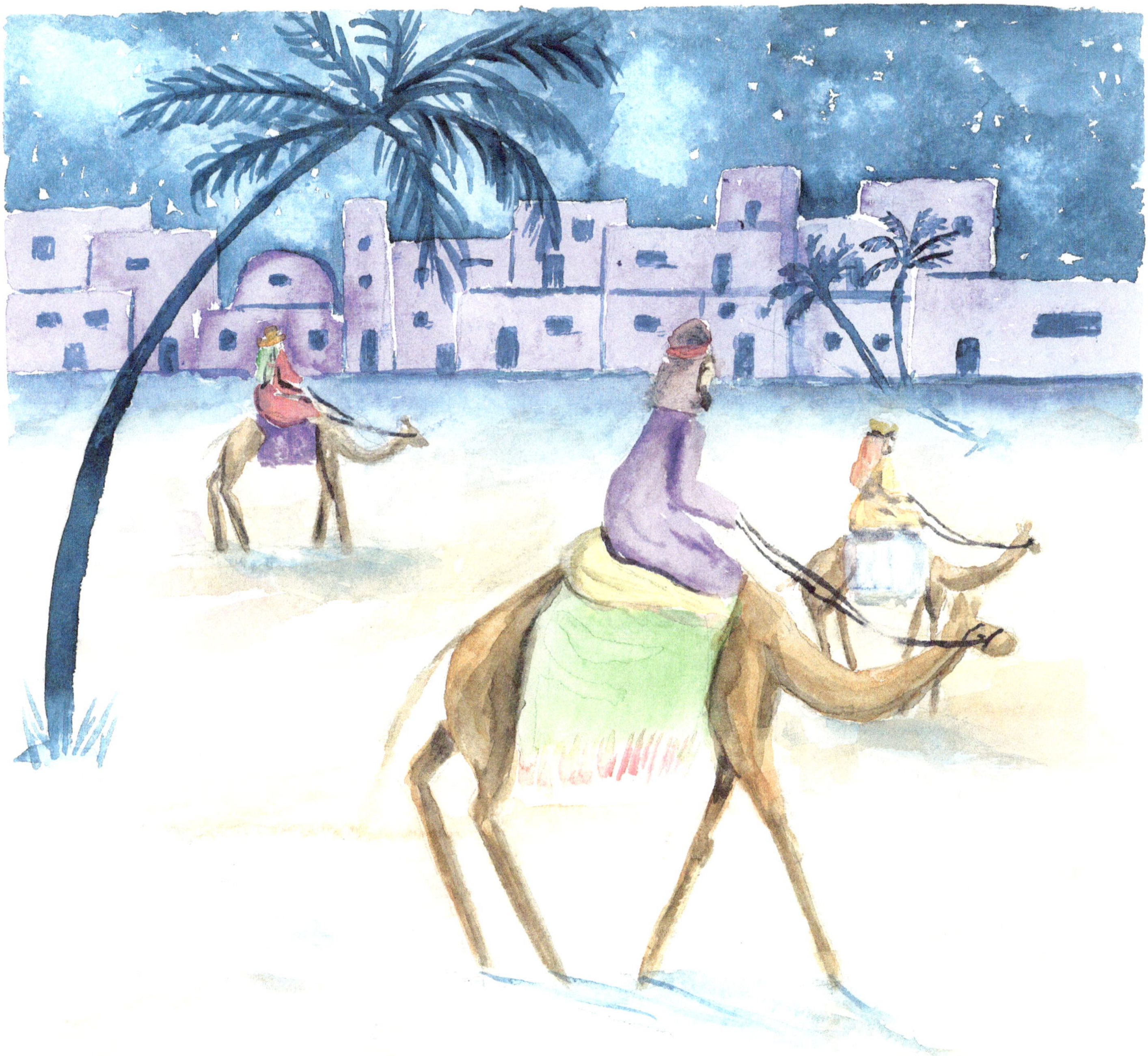

They believed by reading the charts of the heavens that this little child could possibly be a newborn king! They couldn't waste any time!

In those ancient times, we are told they came from the East. This is a region that we identify in today's modern world as the Middle-East.

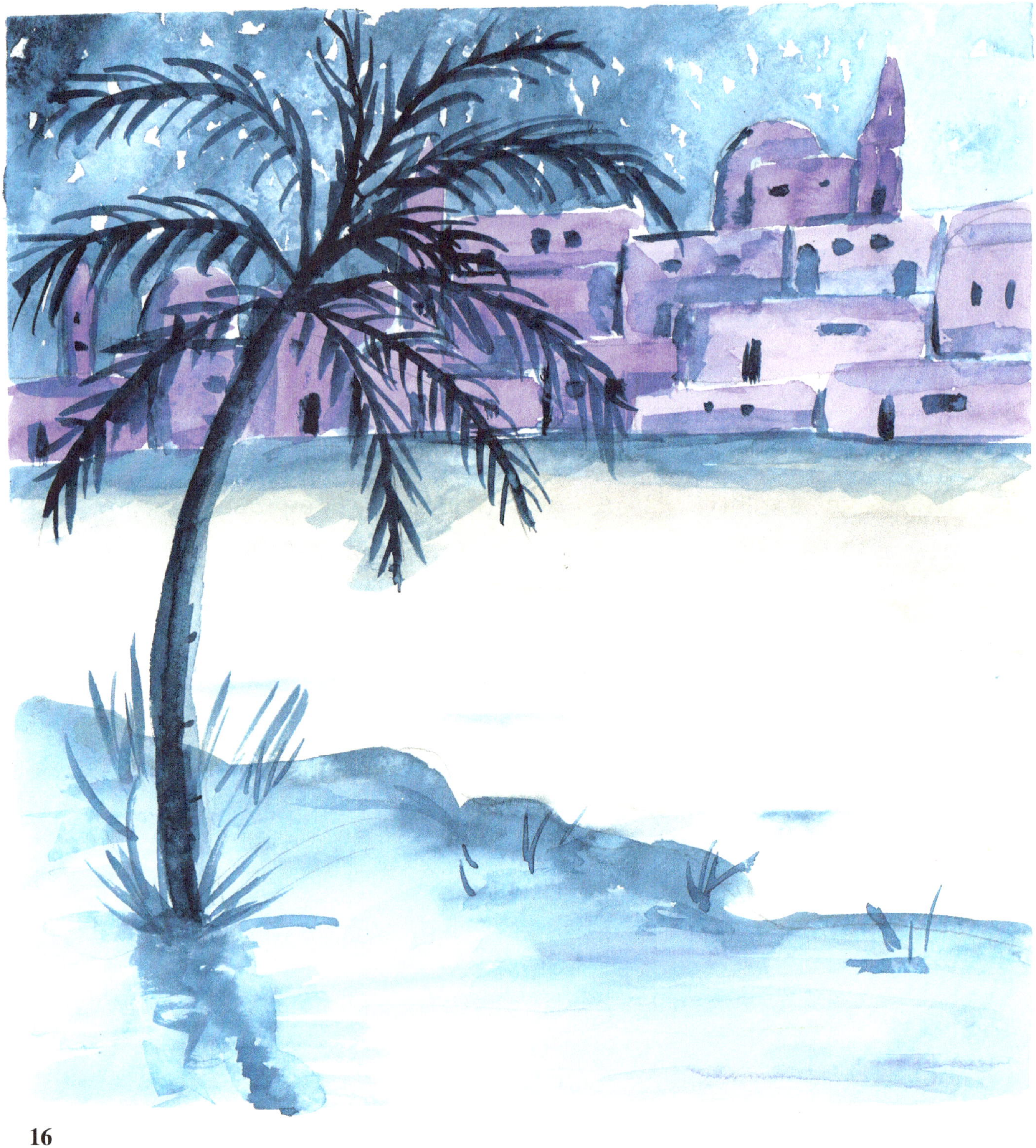

After many, many days and nights of travel they found themselves in the city of Jerusalem. It was there that they met King Herod.

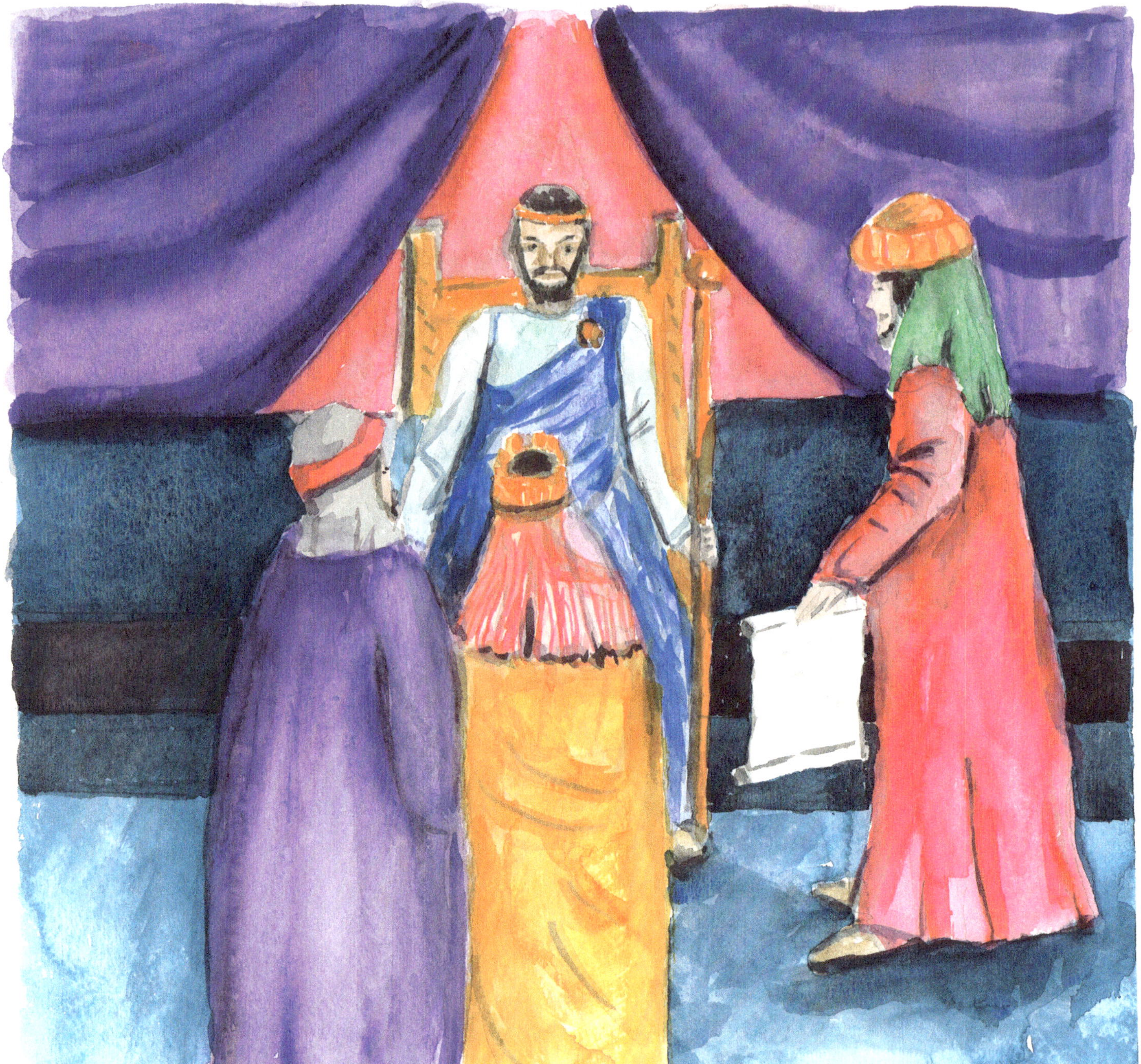

They told King Herod that they believed a new king had been born and they wanted to bring the child royal gifts of gold, frankincense, and myrrh.

Now King Herod was jealous of the new born king, and even a bit threatened, but he disguised his feelings very well. He asked the wise men to bring back word to him of the location of the child, because he too, wanted to celebrate his birth.

But being a bit suspicious of King Herod, the wise men decided not to share that information with him on their return trip. They knew a jealous king when they saw one!

They continued on their journey, and when the star came to rest over the little town of Bethlehem, they were filled with joy!

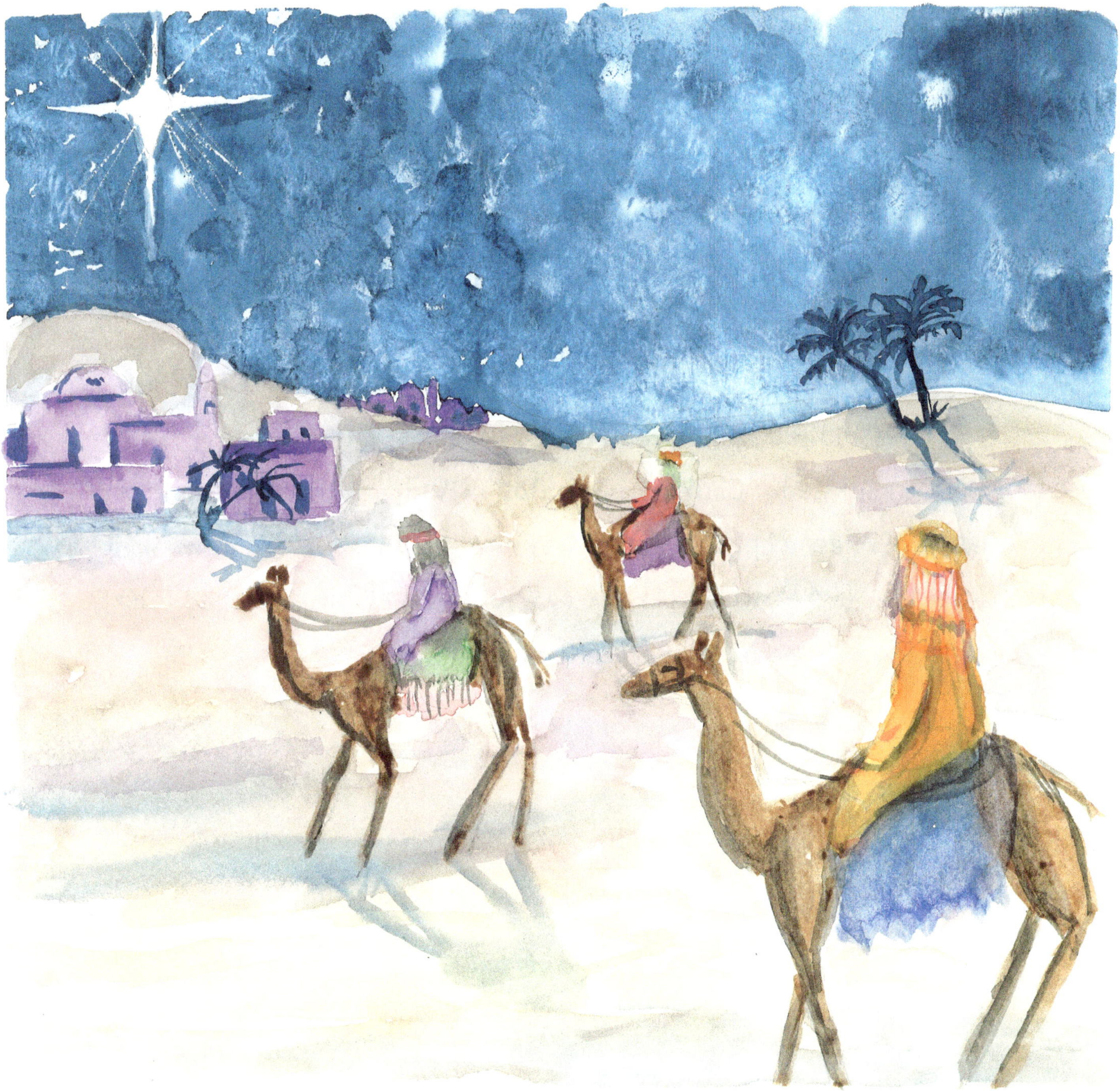

So, how did they know where to go? That's why this book is called "Coulda', Woulda', Did!" There are at least three explanations. When you look at them you will see that all of them work. Which one helped the wise men? You can decide for yourself.

25

First, there are those who believe it happened quite naturally.* What we mean by that is that some things occur in the heavens that are quite natural. Maybe the Christmas star was a comet. Comets are like shooting stars and can be viewed over a period of time.

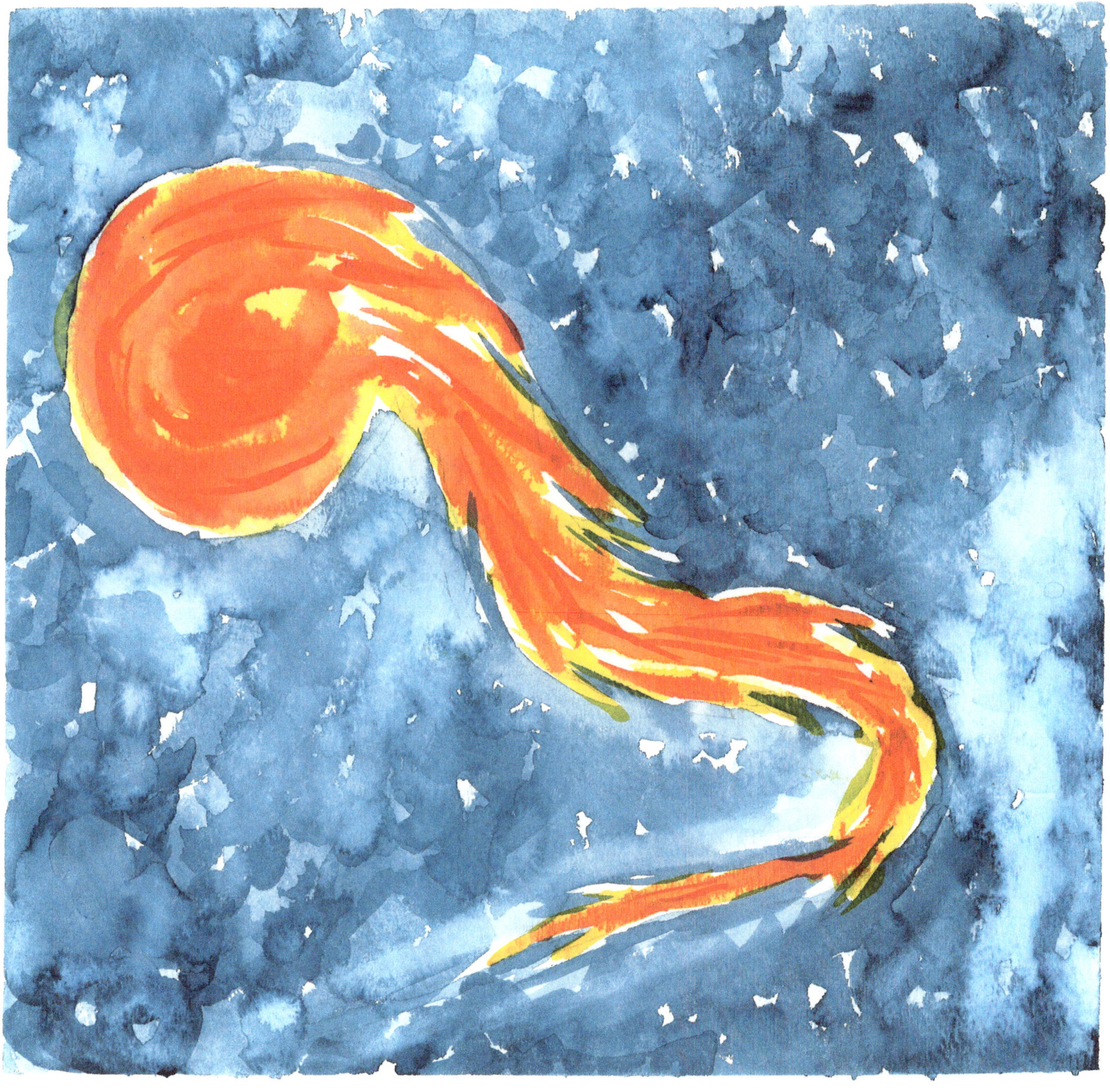

There also could have been a supernova in the heavens then. A supernova is a group of stars that come close together and such a thing has happened a number of times in the history of the world.

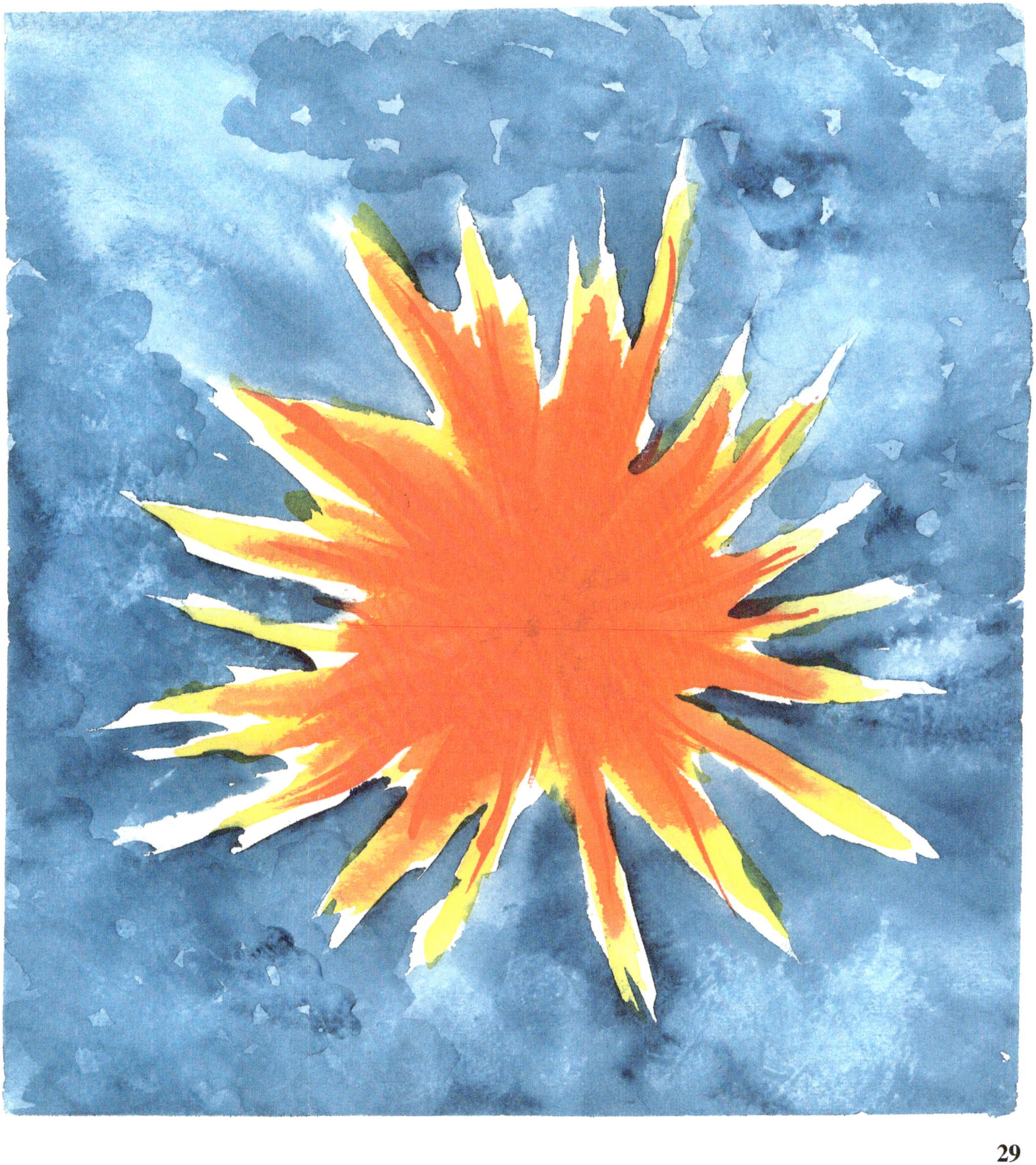

It is also believed that several planets in the solar system could have been in just the right alignment and the wise men could have noticed something like that!

31

Any of these *natural* things could have happened at the time that Jesus was born. If that was the case…it would have been *natural*…and that coulda' led the wise men to the baby Jesus.

Secondly, others think that the star was a *supernatural* event.** In other words, if God wanted to use a certain star in a certain way, then God is powerful and mighty enough to do just that!

And, if God used a **supernatural** way of leading the wise men, it's possible they...were the ONLY ONES who saw the star! That would have been **supernatural** and that woulda' led them to the baby Jesus.

But there is one more idea, and it is the third idea. Perhaps there is an angelic explanation.***

If an angel first told Mary that she would give birth to a special baby,

And if an angel told Joseph, her husband not to be afraid for Mary's sake,

And if the angels announced to the shepherds when they were out on a hillside keeping watch over their sheep, that the Son of God had been born,

Then, why couldn't an angel lead the wise men to Jesus? And if we understand it that way, then an angel... *did*...have something to do with it. The guiding star, in turn, became a guiding angel!

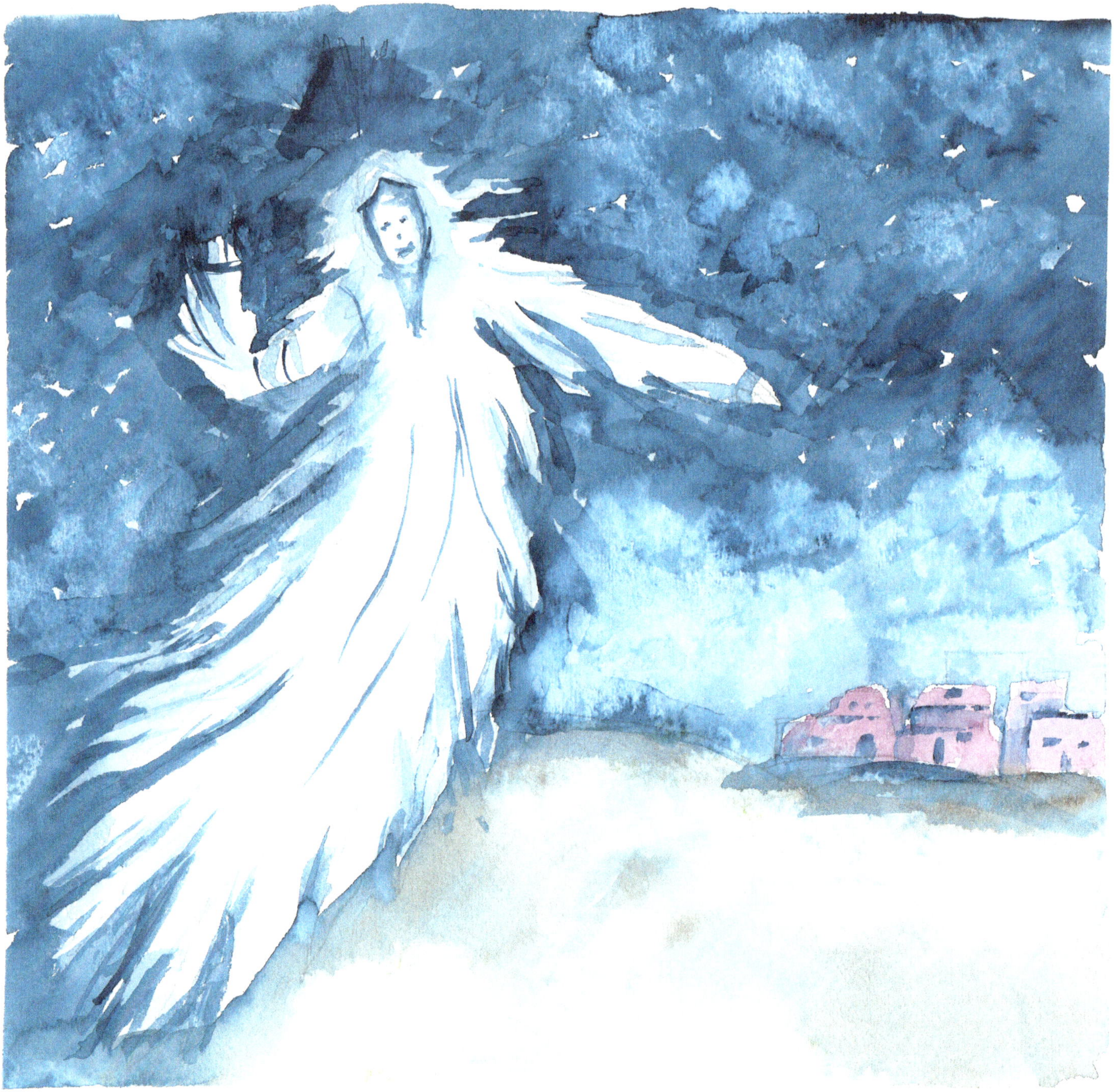

Coulda',...Woulda',...Did! No matter how it happened, our hearts are glad for the Christmas star and the coming of Jesus into the world!

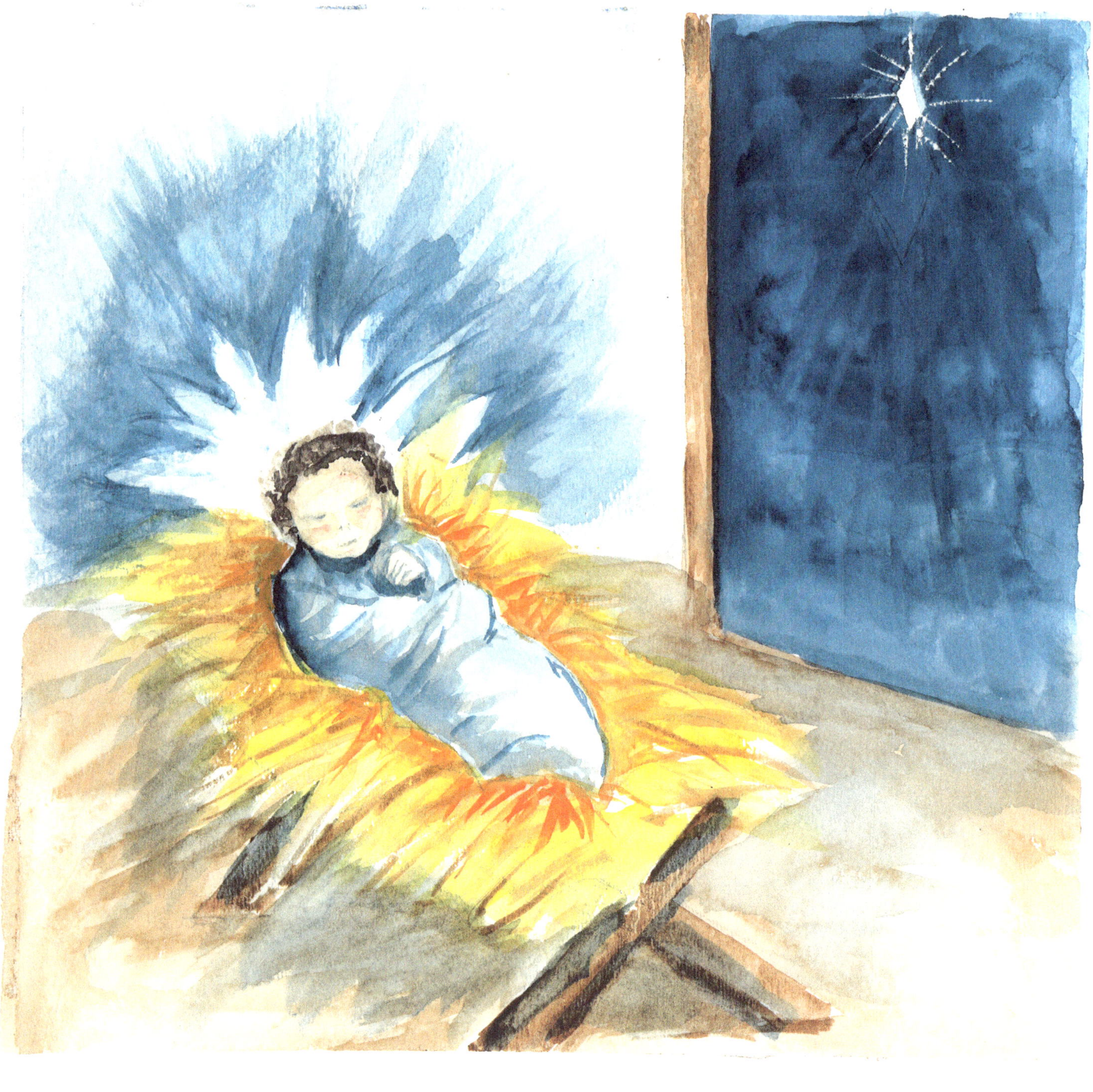

Notes to parents:

* Many suggest that it was a natural phenomenon that can be traced back to some known, periodically occurring, astronomical event. We know, for a fact that Halley's Comet was visible in 12 and 11 B.C. A supernova or a conjunction of planets may be another explanation. One widely discussed possibility is an unusual conjunction of planets that occurred on May 27, 7 B.C. According to this theory, Jupiter represented the primary deity in Babylonian astrology. When Jupiter came close to Saturn (representing the Jews) in Pices, (the constellation representing Palestine) the magi (wise men) referred to Jupiter as the star of the king they were seeking, and the association of Saturn and Pices showed them, exactly where to look. Jupiter rose on March 11, 7 B.C., so this would have been the date when the star of the Christ arose. One astronomer concludes that the conjunction alerted the wise men to some unusual appearance and the supernova triggered their journey to Jerusalem. If this theory is true, then this natural phenomenon "coulda'" accomplished what God wanted done.

** Others suggest that the "star" was a supernatural astral phenomenon that God used to announce Jesus' birth. Note in the Matthew 2:9 account of the scriptures how it appears and reappears, as well as moves the wise men to the very house that Jesus and his family were occupying. This is not the normal activity of stars. Some conclude that this star-like phenomenon would have only been seen by the wise men and no one else! This most certainly "woulda'" led them to Jesus.

*** Another plausible suggestion is that an angel was sent to the wise men to announce the birth of the Messiah and to guide them to Jesus so they would be a witness to his birth through their worship. Some angels, who perform especially important acts are commonly referred to as stars in Hebrew literature. Angels were used to guide Israel to the Promised Land (Exodus 14:19 and 23:20).

The apocryphal Arabic Gospel of the Infancy relates Matthew's account of the wise men, but expands it to say, "In the same hour there appeared to them an angel in the form of a star which had been before them, guiding them on their journey, and they went away, following the guidance of its light, until they arrived in their own country."   One biblical scholar concludes, "This, I believe only makes explicit what is implicit in Matthew, namely, the guiding star was…an angel!"

Zondervan illustrated Bible Background Commentary, Vol 1. Clinton E. Arnold, editor

Zondervan Publishing, 2002 p. 16

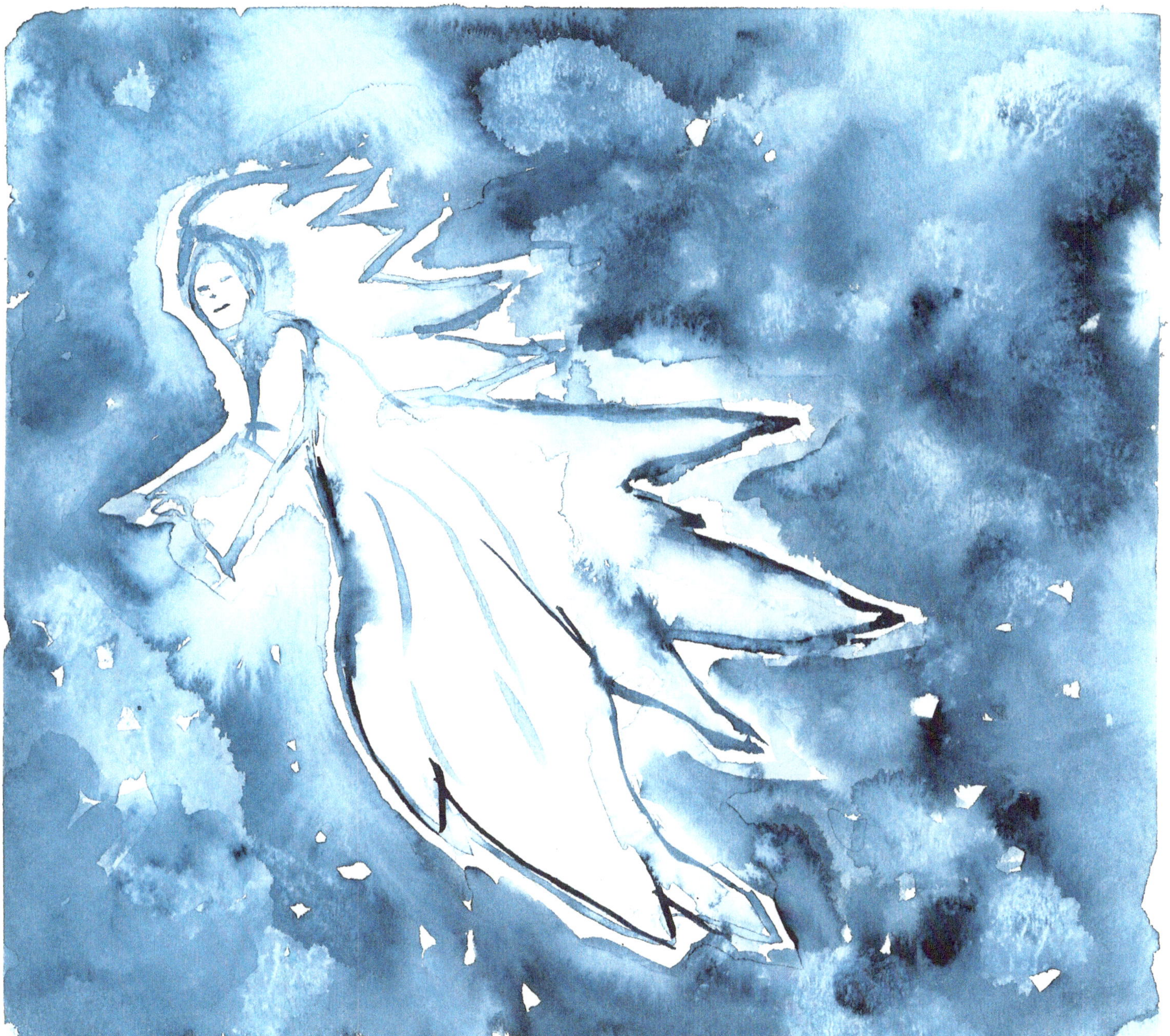